Kydney

By Beth Heath Lee

Trilogy Christian Publishers
A Wholly Owned Subsidiary of Trinity Broadcasting Network
2442 Michelle Drive
Tustin, CA 92780

For information, address Trilogy Christian Publishing
Rights Department, 2442 Michelle Drive, Tustin, CA 92780.
Trilogy Christian Publishing/ TBN and colophon are trademarks of Trinity Broadcasting Network.

For information about special discounts for bulk purchases, please contact Trilogy Christian Publishing.

10 9 8 7 6 5 4 3 2 1

Library of Congress Cataloging-in-Publication Data is available.

ISBN 979-8-89041-420-5
ISBN 979-8-89041-421-2 (ebook)

DEDICATION

This book is dedicated to my parents, Attorney and Mrs. Millard C. Heath Sr. Though their voices are silenced, their memories linger on in my heart and mind forever.

CONTENTS

Acknowledgements 1
Chapter 1 3
Chapter 2 13
Chapter 3 15
Chapter 4 17
Chapter 5 19
Chapter 6 21
Chapter 7 23
Chapter 8 25
Chapter 9 27
Chapter 10 29
Chapter 11 31

ACKNOWLEDGEMENTS

This book would not have been possible without the grace that God poured into my heart to share my story of survival. *Kydney* was born out of my commitment to Him. *Kydney* shares my love, my fears, and my hope for humanity.

I acknowledge that a tinge of fear crossed my mind, but I knew that my sacrifice was for a great cause: to save a life. My hope was that this transplant would improve the quality of my husband's life. He was on dialysis twice a week, and his life was grueling and difficult. My hope for humanity is that we reexamine our priorities and our lives. If we would only become conscious of the foods we put into our bodies, we could decrease the number of people dying from dialysis every day. In addition, there are enough kidneys out there to save many lives if more people would donate their own.

I thank and acknowledge my husband, Roy Edward Lee, Sr., the recipient of my kidney. I also acknowledge my amazing children, my loves, my heartbeats: Roy Lee Jr., Walter Anthony Knowles, Centennial Knowles Dye, and Earl Germaine Lee for their undying support before, during and after the kidney transplant of November 2006. I will never forget how they came together for Thanksgiving and prepared the best Thanksgiving dinner ever. Even my son-in-law and daughters-in-law came out to help. What a tremendous blessing to see them work together and accomplish something so amazing. I am forever grateful.

I acknowledge and am grateful to St. Luke's Hospital in Houston, Texas for taking care of Roy and me during this difficult time. Thank you to every doctor, nurse and staff member who made our stay comfortable and safe. Thank you to the entire transplant team who made the donation a smooth and easy process.

Finally, I acknowledge and thank Kydney for her sacrifice and bravery. Without her, there would not be a book called *Kydney*.

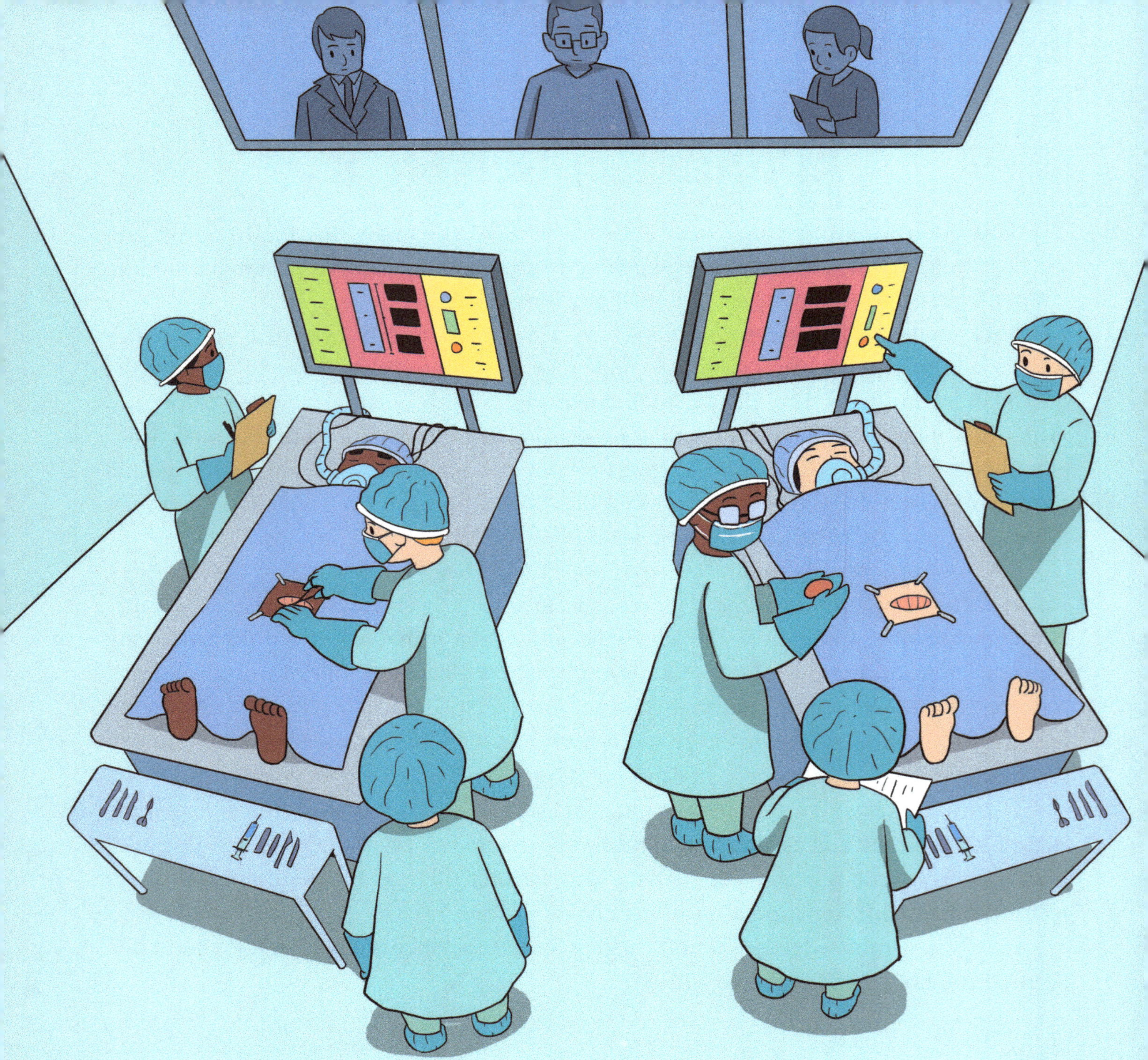

CHAPTER 1

Kydney was abandoned suddenly, and she did not know why. All she felt was that her mother no longer wanted her, and she was given away. Kydney had no say. One day she was functioning normally, and the next thing she knew, she was literally cut out. Who could do that to their child? Kydney was a great child, and just like that, she was snatched away. Kydney thought her mother had to be the most evil person on the planet. She was in a warm and safe place, and suddenly she was snatched away to never see her mother again. This was in November 2006. She now lives in a foreign land. She didn't ask to go; she was taken away. She could hear her mother cry for her, but she knew she would never be close to her again. Kydney was a twin, and she longed to be near her sister, but since her abandonment, she has never seen her sister or her mother again.

Kydney was beautiful, and her mother loved her very much. Her mother gave her up to save another person's life, but Kydney could not understand why. Why her? Why was she chosen? What had she done to deserve this? She used to be happy and safe. She ate the best of foods, and she delighted in the way her mother cared for and nurtured her, but she was sacrificed to go somewhere no child should ever be allowed to go.

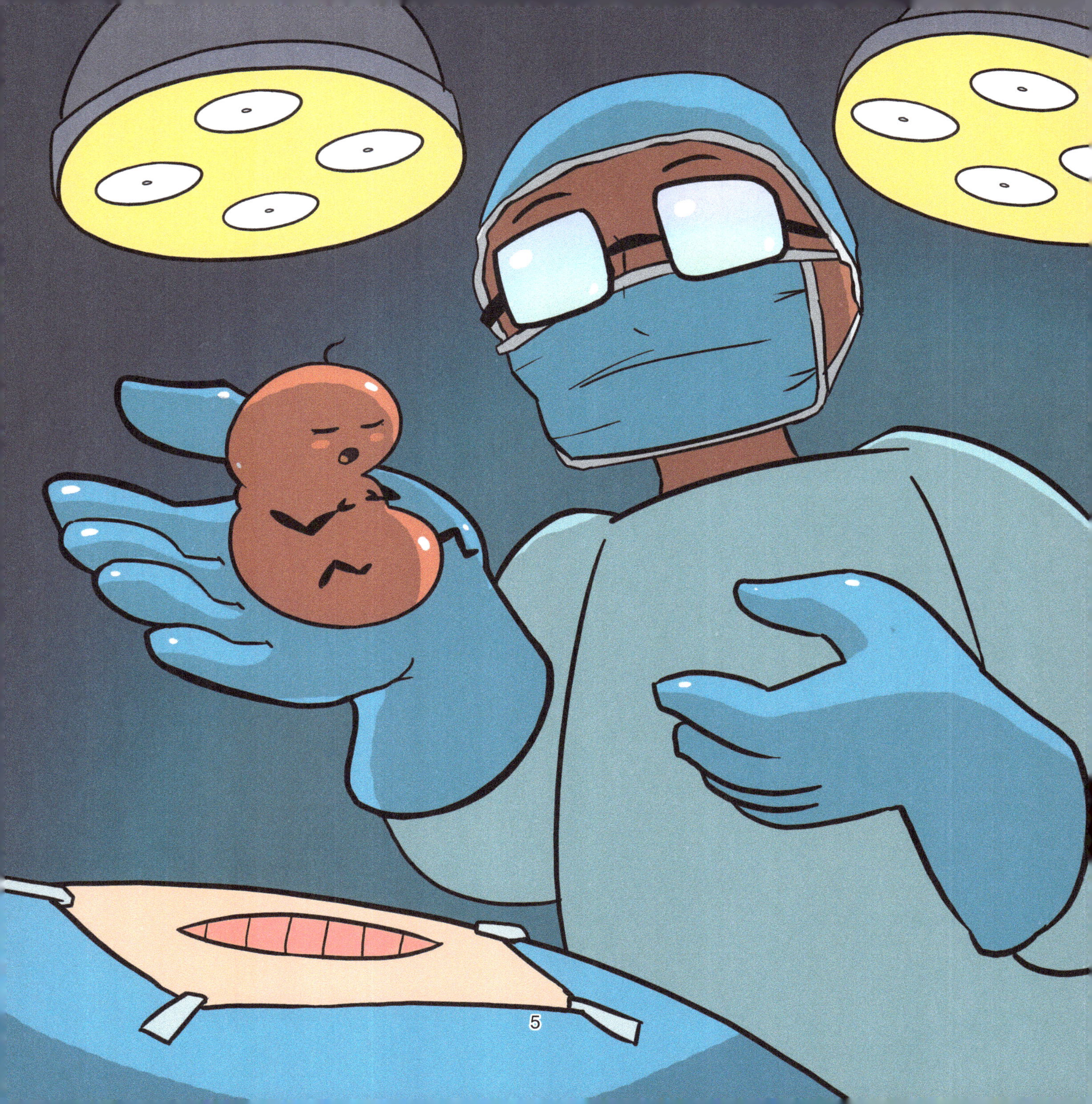

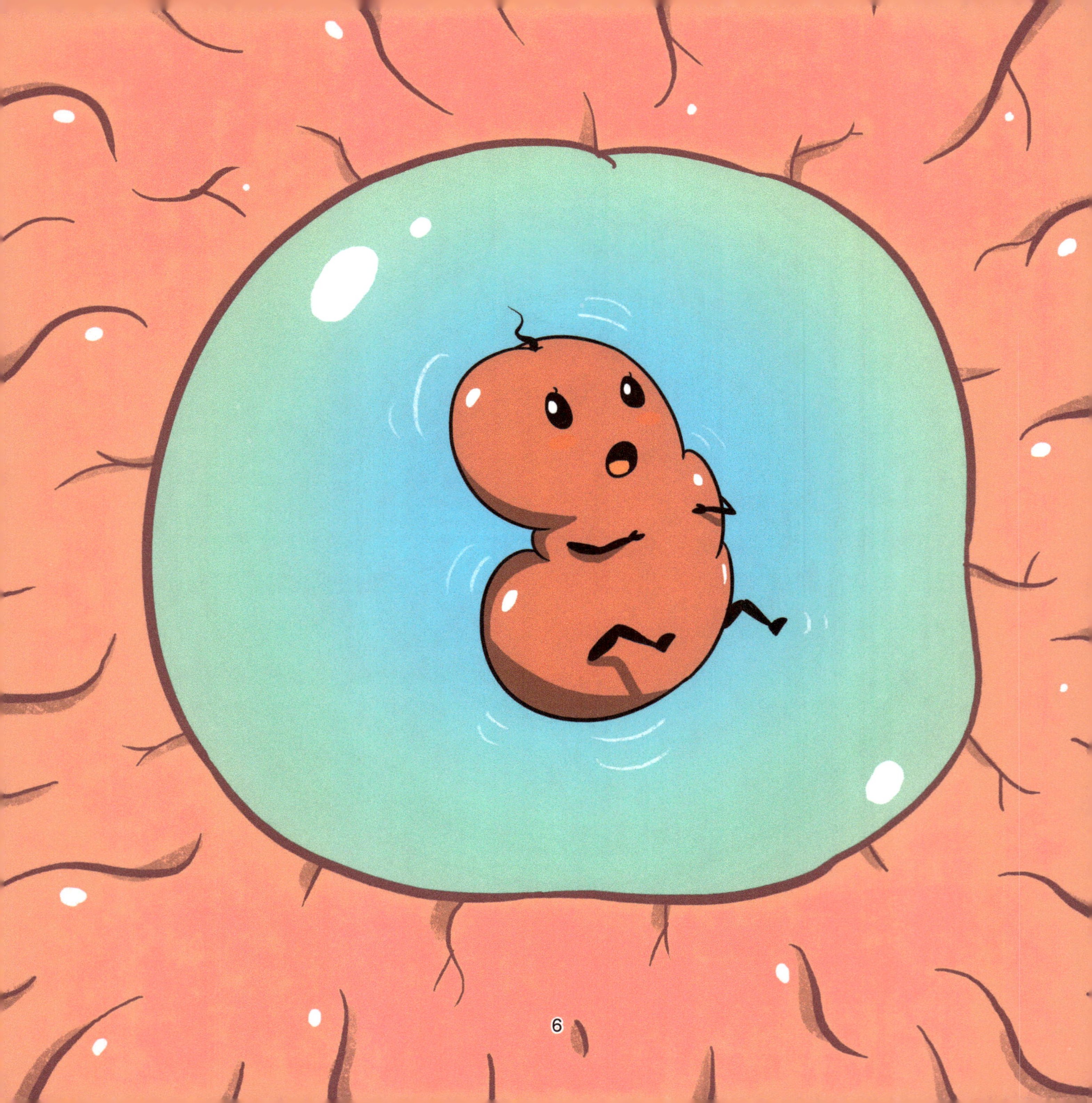

She now lives in the confines of a circular wall. Every day she struggles to survive because her new owner was a master at consuming the wrong kind of food, doing the wrong kinds of things, and not caring what anybody had to say about it. Kydney must work overtime filtering all the dirt and grime that entered her. Her mother knew and saw, but she was helpless for a little while. She knew that Kydney needed her, but she wasn't sure how to help her. Mother needed a plan to save Kydney. She needed a plan to help her thrive in her new environment, so Mother began to orchestrate ways for Kydney's new master to nourish Kydney. However, he didn't always listen. How could Mother help someone who didn't want to listen? Mother had an idea. From this day forward, she would prepare healthy and nourishing meals for him to eat. She would include lots of vegetables, fruits, salmon and chicken. Mother knew that this was the key to Kydney's survival. If he could change his diet, change his choices, and change his mind, Mother could assure that her dear little Kydney would survive.

Little by little, it worked. Kydney got bigger and stronger. Though Kydney worked tirelessly day and night, she became determined to persevere. *I must live*, she thought. It became her mission to survive any obstacle thrown her way. Her body was flooded with many different medicines. She had to consume insulin, diuretics, blood pressure medicines, pain killers, medicines with strange names like Eliquis and Torsemide and Pravastain and names she could not even pronounce. Some days she felt completely drugged and sluggish. Her master loved hamburgers and hot dogs and all sorts of fast food. He loved candies and ice cream and made an assortment of bad choices. Kydney's small body could hardly take the consequences, but she would do whatever it took to live.

Kydney woke up early and stayed up late. She needed to be alert in case Mother came back for her. Deep down inside, she waited for Mother, hoping she would return, embrace her, love her, and never ever let her go again. However, Mother never returned. She was too busy working or cooking or cleaning or taking care of other people's children. *What about me?* Kydney wondered. "What about my life?" Kydney cried! Heartbroken, Kydney tried to get some rest, but rest would not come.

Kydney's new owner was a mean old man, but Kydney figured he couldn't be worse than her mom. She would never have to worry about him giving her away. He was mean because life had made him this way. He was a United States Marine who served in the Vietnam War. He said it was not a pretty war, and he should not have survived. He saw death in its purest form, and it made an indelible impact on his life. He could never forget his experiences. His entire body crumpled under their weight. He lost a kidney, then a foot, then another foot, then a leg, then another leg, then a knee. He had no friends because he was unfriendly, and he had no hope. He needed special care, but Mother refused to let him go to a nursing home. He had served this country, and he deserved to live in the comfort of his own home.

Mother decided to do whatever it took to help this veteran. This way, she would be close to Kydney. This delighted Kydney immensely. *At least mother will be close, and I can hear her voice*, thought Kydney. *Mother may not love me*, Kydney thought, but deep down inside, Kydney still loved Mother.

CHAPTER 2

What happened to him? At first, Kydney thought it was her sister. *It looks a little like me, cute but lifeless*, thought Kydney. *What did he do? Why was he here? Why wasn't he buried?*

Kydney desperately wished her mother could hear her. Kydney had so many questions about life and death: Who made us? Why are we here? Why am I here? Why have I been thrown away like an old rag doll? She wanted to know what she had done wrong. She wanted to know why she was hurt like this, and when her mother would return. Would it be a year or two or three? Would it be forever? Kydney felt she deserved an answer; she felt the least her mother could do was answer her questions and provide some closure, but mother could not hear her. "I want my Mama" cried Kydney. "I want my Mama! Somebody help! Get me out of here!" But, her voice was voiceless.

CHAPTER 3

“Mother, help me!” Kydney cried as loudly as her little body could. “Help me, Mother, or I will surely die.” Mother could not hear. Kydney needed a hug, but there was no hug to be found. “I need you! Where are you? Come and take me back. I’m all alone. Can’t you see I’m in trouble? I’m yours, not his.” *How on earth did I end up here?*” Kydney wondered. *If he didn’t take care of himself, how on earth can he take care of me? My sister and I used to play happily every day, but now I’m all alone with a corpse that looks like me. What did I do to be treated so miserably? What did I say for my very own mother to just toss me away like an old shoe?* “Kids, if you can hear me, listen to your parents; Be good to them, because if they get sick of you, they can just snatch you out and throw you away,” Kydney pleaded. “It can happen; Look at me.” Kydney used to think Mother loved kids, but now she’s not so sure. Afterall, Mother had worked with kids for her whole life; she was a teacher. She loved students; she loved *all* of them, but then, suddenly, just like that *she* was the orphan! *I don’t like it here*, thought Kydney. *It’s so dark and depressing. All I hear all day long is people killing people, violence of all kinds, cruelty and hate for one another. Why can’t I hear positive stuff, fun stuff? Every single day, I hear pointless chatter on CNN that has fogged my brain. I’m not learning anything…* “Mother, come get me *now*!”

CHAPTER 4

Who are they? Kydney wondered as she heard children's voices. She recognized the voices. They sounded like Jo Jo, Payton and Edward. *Have they come for little old me?* "Boys… here I am!" cried Kydney… "Help me! *Please* help me!" The children were so consumed with their iPads and computers that they could not hear. Their excited spirits stirred Kydney and made her want to play. She wanted to run, and she wanted to sing with her cousins, but her voice fell on deaf ears. She knew that Mother loved those boys, but she wanted to warn them that she might snatch them too. *Don't get too close kids…that woman has changed*, thought Kydney.

CHAPTER 5

They say there's a God. I don't know. I don't see Him. I can't feel Him. Between the growling and howling of other organs, I cannot detect another voice. They say He died on the cross for my sins, but that still needs to be revealed to me. They say that all you must do is believe, and you will be saved. Well, I need to be saved. I am enclosed in a circle with a corpse. Perhaps *He* can save me. I'm not sure I can count on dear old Mom, so maybe I need to learn who this God is. Perhaps He has mystical powers and can blow me out of here. Perhaps He has magical hands that might shake me loose. "God, if You are there, I'm calling on You to take care of me." I am so lost. I remember a song called "Amazing Grace." It says "how sweet the sound that saved a wretch like me." Wow! "Well, God, I need some saving, and I know a lot of people who need some saving too, Mother included. Perhaps You can get me out of here!"

CHAPTER 6

I'm in a barrel. How could God possibly get to me? When I look up, all I see is blackness. When I look down, all I see is blackness. Where is the light?

Is there light in this dark world of sin? I want to see the Bright and Shining Star. I want to see the One who sacrificed His life for me. God, please help me see You. Please help me understand. Help me understand why my mother doesn't love me anymore. Help me understand why I was abandoned and stolen from my family. Help me understand why I'm stuck here in a place I don't want to be. Help me understand this cruel and unjust world we live in. Just help me understand. Talk to me and help me see. I can't talk to my mother. That woman won't give me a straight answer.

CHAPTER 7

This barrel is getting bigger and bigger, and I'm feeling more and more sluggish. He eats *everything*: Pizzas and hamburgers, cookies and cakes, starches and sugars, processed foods, sausages and pork chops, bacon and cheeses. Those giant-sized drinks are drowning me and causing me to gag. People don't have to buy them just because vendors sell them. Why do people eat so much? They are killing themselves. They only get one body. Why don't they take care of that one? I guess I will never know.

CHAPTER 8

I'm not feeling well today. Everything around me is swelling. My head has doubled in size. "Mom, where are you? I need your help." Every time I try to filter my body, something gets stuck. It's too dark for me to see or understand what's going on. "What kind of mother are you? All I know is I need you…again. Please don't be far away. I don't hear your voice… just a medical team discussing the next steps. It seems like someone is angry because I hear so many expletives flying around the room. I'm a helpless child in need of my mother, so where are you? I feel dazed from the extra stuff they are serving me, and this stuff is not food. It's like green slime. I am *starving* Mom. Did you leave me to starve? I want to be near you. I need you to hug me and to love me. I need you to tell me you were *wrong* for giving me up. I forgive you. Will you forgive me? If I did anything to hurt you or disrespect you, please forgive me. Just let me come back home!"

CHAPTER 9

Oh, how wonderful my life was. Every day was a holiday. Mother was such a nice lady. I don't really know when she changed. Every day was so beautiful. I did not have a worry in the world. I did not have any problems with the food I ate nor the drinks I drank. I remember Mother telling me to avoid buffets. She said they were a recipe for disaster. She told me to eat plenty of fruits and vegetables, which she did. She said if you are careful about what you eat, you won't have to worry about dieting. She believed if you eat nutritious foods, you will never have to worry about excess weight. I loved that woman. Now, I must eat whatever comes my way, and fruits and vegetables are not on the menu. I miss the apples, oranges, bananas and strawberries. I miss the carrots, spring mixes, tomatoes and cucumbers. I'm tired now. I need some rest.

CHAPTER 10

I'm feeling better today, Mother. I slept well, and I ate well. I know you will come for me, Mother, so I must preserve my energy and garner some strength. I know you'll return, I just don't know when. You would never really leave me, would you Mom?

I think I heard your voice! I know it's you. I think you're cooking. I recognize the sounds of your pots and pans. I hear music. You always loved listening to spiritual songs as you cooked. This is great, but I need you closer, Mother. You have almost found me. You can't hear me because the pots and music are too loud. Come closer, Mother. I'm calling for you, Mother, amidst the most beautiful music. I hear "How Great is Our God." I hear you faintly in the background. It's you, Mother. I would recognize your beautiful voice anywhere. I love the sound. I hear you talking, but I can't discern what you're saying. "Mother! Mother! Come closer." Stay still. You're moving too much. They used to say you're like the Energizer Bunny, and now I see what they mean. You have almost found me, Mother! Please don't stop looking. I can feel that you are searching for me. *Thank you, God. Please help her find me.* I am so happy now. I feel your presence, Mother. I can't see you, but I feel your spirit all around me. I love you. I will always love you. Mother, you will be so proud of me. I'm not afraid anymore. I feel safe and happy because I know you are searching for me. I'm trying to speak loudly, but you are not responding to my voice. Can you hear me? Why do people think I can't communicate? I *can* hear. Cells are not dead. We eat, we sleep, we drink, and we give signs when something is wrong, and we will talk to you, but you must listen. Mother, you will be so proud of me. Every day I am striving to live. If I live, I have a chance to see you once again. I remember your voice, your words, and your love. You never told me you loved me, but I always knew with all my heart that you loved me, until that fateful day when you decided to give me away. Couldn't you have at least consulted me? Did you think I wanted to go? I would never have left you because I love you, Mother. I have always loved you. Until my last breath, I always will.

Dear Kydney,
I

CHAPTER 11

My dear Kydney,

I love you, and I would never leave you. I have been with you all along. Yes, I know you feel like I abandoned you, but I am here with you and I am for you. Kydney, God gives us life, and through me and you, He provided an opportunity to help save another life. God used us to help Roy, my husband. Kydney, I knew you were very strong. I knew this because you are just like me. You are strong like your mother and like my dear mother, Queen Elizabeth Heath. We were made that way. I knew you were strong, and I needed you to help my husband who was dying from dialysis. He went in for dialysis twice a week, and life for us was very, very bleak. *A new kidney could save his life*, I thought. His kidney had failed. That's the corpse that you see. He was on a kidney transplant list, but time was not on his side. Thankfully, you were the perfect match. Can you believe it? God worked it out so that through you, another soul could live. I thank God for you. Thank you, Kydney, for being so brave and so strong.

Why didn't I ask you? I didn't ask you because I knew you would not want to go. However, you and your twin sister are so astounding that, together, you have sustained two people: me and Roy. I knew we could do this, and we have, and I am so happy and grateful. Thank you, Kydney. Thank you for your role in making this happen.

Many have asked why I didn't just send Roy to a nursing home. How could I have lived with myself if I did that? I am able to care for him! It was about more than him, Kydney. It was about *you*! I did it for you…my very own kidney whom I loved. I have always been there by Roy's side, but once you became a part of him, I became doubly blessed when I cared for him. Every time I fed him, I fed you. Every time I dressed him, I dressed you. Every time I missed him, I missed you. You are amazing, Kydney. I never abandoned you, my dear one. I love you, and I will never leave you.

Now, Kydney, I want to tell you about a God who will never leave you either. Our God is an *awesome* God. He is our creator. Without Him, we would not be here. Without Him, there would not be any little boys or little girls. God created the entire universe. He created birds and bees and *every* living thing on this earth. He created all the other planets, too. Isn't that *amazing*? Everything you see on Earth came from God. He made all of us, and He knows all about us. He loves us unconditionally. My dear Kydney, please don't ever forget this. He cares so much for us that He knows the number of hairs we have on our heads. Isn't that incredible? Never forget that God is always there. We are never alone. We may *feel* alone, but He is *always* with us. Baby, God loved us so much that He gave His only begotten Son, so that "whosoever believeth in Him shall not perish but have everlasting life (John 3:16)". Jesus Christ died on a cross on a hill called Calvary for your sins, for my sins, and for the sins of this world. Jesus Christ was sacrificed for all of us. Through Him, we have an opportunity to receive everlasting life.

Kydney, you have been wonderfully and beautifully made. God loves you, and so do I.

Love,
Mother

To be continued…

ABOUT THE AUTHOR

Beth Heath Lee is the daughter of Attorney Millard C. Heath and Queen Elizabeth Heath. She was born on December 20, 1951 in Galena Park, Texas. She attended and graduated from Fidelity Manor High School in May of 1969. She is a proud member of the class of '69. She attended Texas Southern University where she received her bachelor's (1973) and master's (1974) degrees in secondary education. She taught school in the North Forest Independent School District, the Houston Independent School District, and surrounding areas for over thirty years. In addition, she served as School Coordinator under the illustrious leadership of Mr. Bill McCluskey at the Juvenile Detention Center when it was located on West Dallas in Houston, Texas. She also served as Reading Supervisor in the Houston Independent School District.

Beth Heath Lee is currently married to Roy Edward Lee, a disabled Vietnam Marine who does not have legs or feet. He spent a couple of years on dialysis before she donated one of her kidneys to him in November of 2006. They have been married for forty-one years. Mrs. Lee also has four children, of whom she is very proud: Roy Lee Jr., Walter Anthony Knowles, Centennial Knowles Dye, and Earl Germaine Lee. She has the best grandkids on the planet.

Printed in the USA
CPSIA information can be obtained
at www.ICGtesting.com
LVHW062150230224
772660LV00014B/304

9 798890 414205